DEPARTMENT SETUP DURING PRE-OPENING OF NEW HOTEL

HOW TO SET THE DEPARTMENT DURING AN PRE-OPENING PHASE OF THE HOTEL

ANKIT TIWARI

Copyright © Ankit Tiwari
All Rights Reserved.

ISBN 979-888569008-9

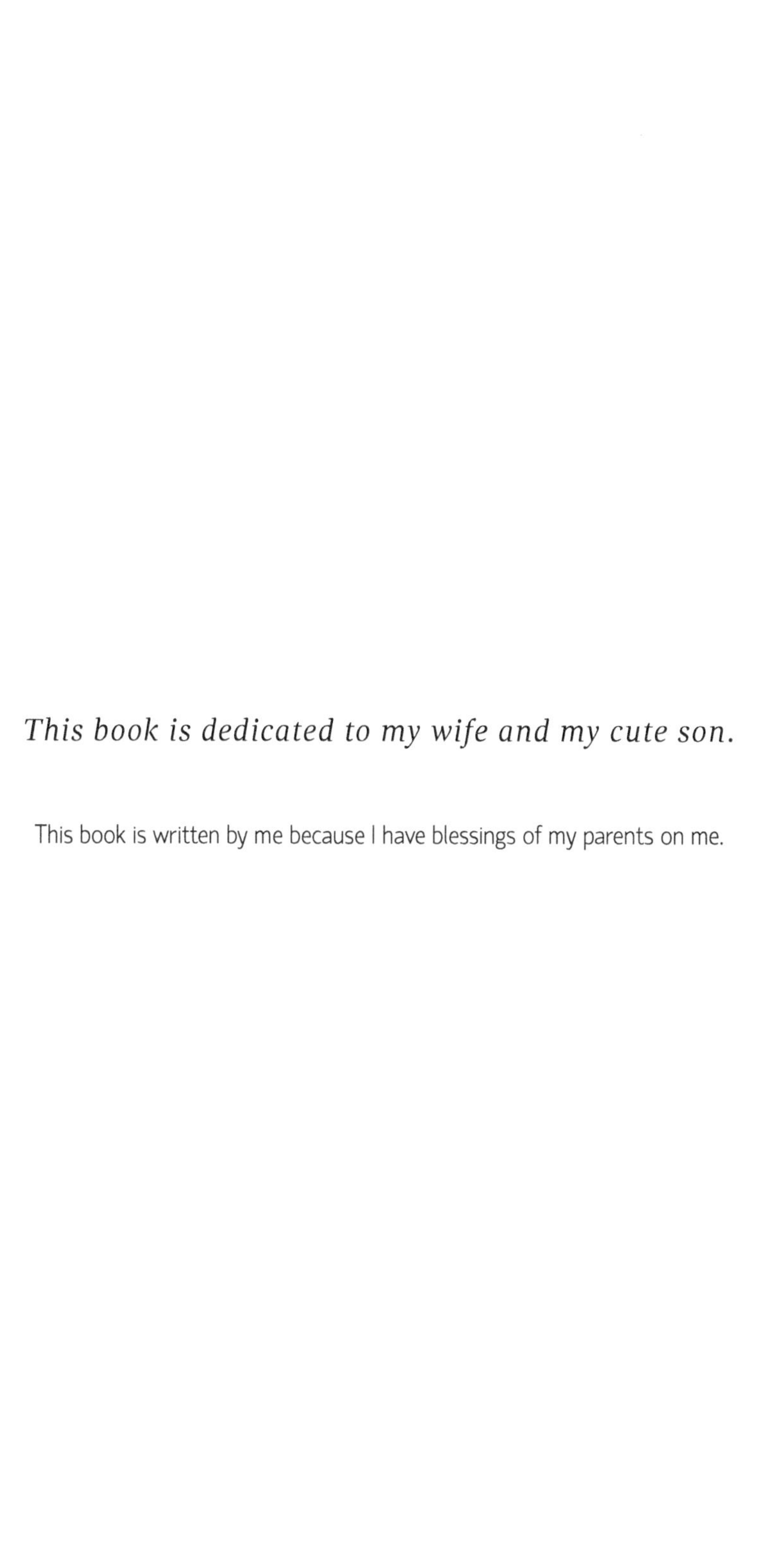

This book is dedicated to my wife and my cute son.

This book is written by me because I have blessings of my parents on me.

Contents

Foreword

The author of this book, Ankit Tiwari is a seasoned hospitality professional, who has vast experience in the hospitality industry. He has a strong background of Front Office department, and knowledge of the different areas of the department such as Cashier, Telephone Operator, Concierge, Duty Manager and Guest Relations. He has worked in the famous hospitality brands such as Taj hotels (IHCL), Radisson Hotel Group (RHG), Intercontinental Hotels Group (IHG), Sarovar Hotels.

The longest tenure spent by the author was with Taj Hotels, which was almost nine years. Feather in the cap was Rambagh Palace, Jaipur where the service was for six years.

Preface

Since the author has experience in pre-opening team at various designations and couple of destinations, so tried to pen down this and thought of sharing his knowledge and experience with the budding hospitality professionals and acquaintances, and obviously with the students, who wish to pursue their career in this industry.

In this, author is explaining in detail the steps and procedures for setting up Front Office department during the opening phase of a new hotel.

CHAPTER ONE

Understanding the Department

The very first day when you reach to the hotel, you may feel a little strange. This happens with human mind because when we see new faces and new people, our mind goes haphazard.

When you complete your joining formalities in Human Resource department, you need to ask the Human Resource personnel about your department.

Few questions as a manager you need to ask, just like the same way when the mother is taking her baby to pediatrician, about ailment, medicines, curing period etc.

Questions related to the department like:

a. What is the total manning approved for the department?
b. What is the break-up of the manning at each designation?
c. What is the total salary range for each member in the team?
d. What is the total salary budget for the department?
e. Any rules for hiring of Fixed Term Contract employee or permanent employee?
f. Any policy related to additional manpower which includes On The Job Trainee (OJT) and Industrial Exposure Trainees (IET)?
g. Did Human Resources personnel hire someone before the joining date of the department Head?
h. Does the Department Head have any flexibility in manipulating salary at any designation, based upon the candidate?

i. Did the candidate who joined before joining of the department Head, has completed the joining formalities of the company?
j. Was the recruited candidate briefed about the department, job description and work schedule?

After all these discussions and queries, if in case any other topic or question that can be solved or discussed during regular work routine as well.

Now it's time to take a look of your department or *you may say your baby child*, in person.

How it has been designed by the engineers and architects? What thing would be fixed or kept at which location? How your team can be seated and accommodated comfortably?

At the end of the day this department and your team has to work there, and they are your reason of growth and development, so you need to take care of them very well. *Treat your team members as your own sons and daughters.*

You may never get the department in a finished look or as a completed product.

You may need to do small amendments and modifications always as per you and your team convenience (in designing and fixtures). Sometimes you may require these amendments and modifications on a bigger extent.

****

Meeting the People

Since you have completed the formalities and you have taken round of your department and seen the area from your eyes, now the time has come to meet the people of your department, if any.

Else take the round of the property and meet people from different departments and make them aware about your presence.

If you happen to meet people from your team, then have a good and healthy interaction.

Let them know who you are and also make them aware about yourself, simultaneously, know them also with detailed introduction. It will make your bonding strong with them.

"Sometimes knowing about an individual makes the conversation interesting".

You need to know the individual(s) who were hired by the Human Resource, because then you need to strategise your work, and use their energy in the right direction to make the operations smooth.

You need to know their knowledge, experience, family, intelligence and their awareness about the job.

On the very first day of meeting with them, let them be at ease and settle down, but at the same time they need to be apprised about discipline which they need to follow in the department during the operations.

Since you have joined the department, now you need to justify your salary from the first day. For that justification, start giving the task to the team member, based upon his knowledge and experience.

If nobody has been hired by the Human Resource, you need to sit and plan your days and strategise your work a day prior, on daily basis.

Planning in a new setup does not mean planning in air, it means sit down and write in diary and plan your work daily.

****

CHAPTER THREE

Mindset

So, now you are clear that your Human Resource department was waiting for you in building your team, so you need to tie your shoes tightly because now it's time to get your people and build a team. The team which is strong enough, and ready to share the shoulder for upcoming responsibilities.

Now you need to look for sources that can help you in getting the people. Sources such as your own acquaintances, print media, social media, job search portals, hotel schools and from other departments, and don't forget to knock the door of your Human Resources department.

It is easy these days that the technology helps us in many ways. You may share your requirements and you may expect responses. People are very active on social media these days.

You need to hire someone and you are looking for it on macro level then make your organization and yourself visible on social media and simultaneously on print media like newspaper.

By newspaper, I mean to express all newspapers if possible, local or national, so that you can reach to maximum people.

You need to talk to people and understand the mindset for hiring the people. Sometimes you don't get responses on social media post(s), so you need to understand by talking to them. You need to know what the expectations of people are and what they are looking for their growth and future prospects.

Once I opted to join a hotel in a city where there was no branded hotel. The hotel which the company was opening was the first international branded hotel. People of that city were little skeptical as to how the five star international branded hotel work, how the people will work, how to get employed with such hotels, salaries must be very high in such international branded hotels etc..

There are no hotel management colleges in that city so people are less aware about such course, so it was difficult and challenging for recruitments.

Many a times it happened that people working in non- branded hotels on reputed designations, walked in for interviews to get job on entrant or supervisory level. We had to sometimes approach and speak to people in good branded hotels of other neighboring cities within state or different state. We offered them salary hike and better designation so that they can join the hotel.

That's how we changed the mindset of people and citizens of the city while opening of this hotel and it was successfully launched in the city.

****

CHAPTER FOUR

Naming and Categorizing the Product

Why do we have to name and categorize all the products that we manufacture or produce and intend to sell?

To make our product stand out in the market and to give a distinct place and identity.

In the case of hotels, we need to name our restaurant(s), bar(s), banquet hall(s), and sometimes the suite(s). In the branded hospitality organizations, we get guidelines on which we need to work and we cannot or you can say we are not allowed to deviate from the standards.

For that matter, not even allowed to change any name and introduce any new thing.

As in starting, I introduced myself about my career journey; I was part of pre-opening hotels, so one of our colleagues suggested the name of the restaurant in that new property. That was supposed to be a multi-cuisine restaurant. So that name was sent to the corporate office through email, but we received regret from them, because the company had already decided the name of such restaurant across the chain.

Is it just the name of the product? No, it's a brand which the company wishes to promote in the market.

The categorisation is done basically for the rooms based upon its view, bed type, brand of the hotel, type of clientele you wish to cater etc. The categorisation of the room such as Smoking Room,

Front Facing Room, Deluxe room, Corner room etc. This is a process in which the company distinguishes the product within the company, within the competitor, within the city.

These are just the marketing techniques to sell your product to the potential guests, in this competitive market, in the best available manner to earn maximum revenue.

Each and every room, all dining outlets, banquet halls are named and categorised, to give choices to the customers and showcase as the best and distinguished product in the market.

All the names of F & B outlets and the room numbers are noted and require approval from owning company as well as your corporate office team.

Before approving, both the parties (owning company and corporate office team) decide and check on all the parameters. It may take days and weeks to finalise them.

After all this is done, now new task of getting the signages placed on designated walls and areas. Again, the design of signages needs to be approved from both the above mentioned parties.

In heritage properties, one can find the signature suites. This thing I saw during my career journey as well. The suites were named as per the city, the heritage culture (if any), the décor and some suites were even dedicated to the Maharajas and Maharanis. This is nothing, but to add value to the product and, enhance the product.

You must have studied few categories of room(s) in your books during your hotel management course, but these days the categorisation is more than the books, sometimes.

****

CHAPTER FIVE

Software, Computer, Peripherals and Configuration

So after completing naming and categorization, now we need to decide and finalise the product, room tariff, menu pricing, designing of menu etc.

This needs to be done at this stage because we are in 21st century and we rely on the technology and work with the machines. The machine is known as *Computer* and nerve which runs this machine is the *Technology*.

These both science inventions help in running the smooth operations at any hotel.

If we talk about the rooms, then we already finalized and got approvals on category of rooms and room numbers.

Before we feed anything on computer, which is visible to us but not to the guest, needs to be checked and rechecked. The areas which needs to be checked are the amenities available in the room, facilities available in the room, size of the room, view from the window, any special feature of the room etc., These aspects will result in the pricing of the room, which may be based upon the competition, target market*, city, location, brand, spending capacity of the potential guest etc.

Don't worry about the Property Management System (*PMS: as in books*) installation. It was done by the Corporate Information

Technology department.

You just need to fill up the box of PMS now, since, you have prepared all the stuffing material of the empty box of PMS. You need to have regular meeting with PMS Implementation team.

This is not one day task, believe me. It takes a week or more than that, only to configure the settings related to Front Office.

As a Front Office personnel we need to create rooms, room features, size of each room, room name coding, rate/tariff of each room, code of each rate/tariff, taxation, special requests which may arise from guest's side, break up of room categories, likes and dislikes etc.

Ufff.... Its long list to configure!!

This configuration needs to be checked again by the PMS Implementation team because one small mistake can lead to errors and can lead to blunders in reports and also may affect the revenues in later stage.

Never leave the configuration and data feeding in PMS task on your team member, because it is meant to be done by the Manager only. It is highly sensitive and critical task. Giving or delegating this task may increase your workload and it may consume more time.

After you complete this configuration, you need to configure the formats of Front Office on PMS, which would be helpful to the team during the operations.

Let's move on to that part in next chapter!!

**Target market: the market or the guest which you are planning to cater, may vary as per age, demographic, geographic, gender etc.*

****

CHAPTER SIX

Configuration-Formats

If you are working with a brand then don't worry about formats, because the formats are all accredited by your corporate office Information Technology, and PMS Implementation Team is aware about it. They have everything available readily in PMS.

You just need to update your property details such as address, contact details, tax registration number and if you want to reflect the name of owning company, your property features and amenities on certain documents such as brochures and tariff cards etc.

I worked with three brands in pre-opening team, and, I myself got only few changes rest remains same like company name and logo, standard colors, standardized stationary and formats such as registration card, vouchers, accounting books, registers and menu etc.

In non-branded hotels you can take the base of formats of all such documents, as listed below. These formats need to be printed with the help of printing machines:

1. Guest Registration card
2. Baggage tags
3. Car parking tags
4. Log books
5. Order taking register
6. Key jacket
7. Guest request register
8. Message tracking register

9. Wake call register
10. Left/ Lost luggage register
11. Bell desk control register
12. Errand card
13. Paging boards/Placard
14. Paid out voucher
15. Allowance voucher
16. IOU voucher
17. Amenities voucher
18. Business center bill book
19. Travel desk bill book (if not outsourced)
20. Cash receipt
21. Foreign currency Encashment register
22. Cash handover Sheet/register
23. Miscellaneous voucher
24. Concierge control Sheet
25. Shift checklist
26. Inventory register (for different departments)
27. Car checklist
28. Reports on PMS

  a. Upgrade report
  b. Arrival report
  c. Guest In- House Report
  d. Departure report
  e. Allowance Report
  f. Early check in Report
  g. Late departure report
  h. Rate variance report
  a. No Show report
  j. Cancellation report
  k. Credit card settlement repor
  l. Cashier report/sheet
  m. Travel Desk report (Guest Pick and Drop details)
  n. Trace Report

o.   Night Audit report (Most Important)

Some of the formats may be computer generated, depends on your organization. It actually saves your printing cost and you can print through computer with help of PMS during the operations, on normal A4 size paper.

Generally non-branded hotels and few other brands are using IDS (Internet Distribution System) as PMS, because it is cost-efficient and has easy installation charges, whereas majorly international hospitality companies use Opera and Micros as PMS.

All set to go now for the next stage of pre-opening phase.

You climbed one more step of your tenure.

"Your ladder of success has no limits. Keep Climbing".

****

CHAPTER SEVEN

Listing of Property

You have set all your formats and vouchers.

You are all set with guest documents and internal usage documents, now the manager has to list the hotel to publicize and to let the people know about the hotel.

How to do all this? Is it really important? Is it really sensitive job, as heard about it?

This one needs to be done by manager only not by any other team member.

Not at all affordable!!

The reason for not delegating this job to any team member, are as below:

1. Marketing aspect is involved
2. Brand image of the organization
3. It may involve USP of your new property, which cannot be missed at all
4. Important information about the products, such as room, restaurant, recreation facilities and contact information etc.
5. Tariff and Taxation

Listing of property on various portals is mandatory in 21st century, because these days the smart phone and internet are part of our daily life and up to certain extent, life is made convenient by these two inventions of science.

The process of listing seems very easy but it's not that easy, because still companies believe in old school style of filling forms.

You need to have the contact details of the companies on which websites you wish to list. You need to request them for registration forms. In these from you need to fill the details of entire property and the organization. Some companies may ask for the manager details that would be in direct contact at the hotel.

Some of the companies provide you electronic forms which you can fill over the computer and verify by scanned signature of concerned authority.

Some companies provide tabs or space to upload these scanned forms or you may send them over the email address, of so called "Relationship Manager" or "Market Manager".

Once you sent this form then you need to follow up and show your property "Live", because after sending, it may take a week or couple of weeks to show the property "Live" or "Selleable".

It may be so that few details need updating after the property is visible over the portal. To make the property visible and to do changes you are provided with Admin Login and Password.

Because of this login and password you can manage he inventory and rates of your property.

One of the prominent website for all the hotels, where you need to list and the reviews of that portal are really looked upon, is "TRIPADVISOR".

They actually check the genuineness of all the information you provide. While listing your property, you need to be aware of the percentage commission which you would be paying to that company, upon selling the rooms of your hotel.

Oh!! I forgot to mention, that these companies are also called "Online Travel Agents".

Actually these OTA's are also sometimes your sales people for your hotel. They are actually contributing a lot in your room business. Generally they have almost 56% to 66% contribution in a decent business property, during our times.

Don't you think it is a remarkable contribution!

Now coming back to commission percentage the hotels generally pay 20% to 25% commission to each OTA. This is decided by your Corporate Revenue team and no worries at the hotel.

As a manager, the responsibility lies on your shoulder and your reservation staff, that these OTA's do not loosen the end, which in return may reduce the business and probably low in contribution also.

It happened with us in a hotel that one of the OTA was not contributing in revenue and they were generating hardly 2% to 5% contribution among all OTAs.

I was in regular touch with them and they were trying to twist us by asking for increase in commission percentage .Our corporate team told me not to increase any percentage to any OTA. Then corporate team gave me idea to put promotion on that OTA to pick the occupancy and contribution percentage from that OTA.

In other words, we twisted them around and got good results after four months. Although convincing the OTA and implementing of the strategy was not easy, as I wrote here.

Once the listing is done, the property is visible; the key to this safe is with the hotel and the OTA, both the parties. To keep the control in your hand, you may change the admin password. Now you own this portal, manage it and sell it as per your strategies and your tactics.

Mind it the opening date of the property and making the property Live on OTAs should be same else, the sellable date on OTA should be after one day only.

The Live date on OTA should also be same as Live date of your PMS. If everything is same then you are ready to invite your guests as all the *DOORS ARE OPEN*.

****

CHAPTER EIGHT

Equipments Procurement

Ok, the system is ready, formats are ready, but have you checked about other equipments, which you would be requiring to run the operations.

Equipments such as Electronic Data Capture (EDC) machine(s), Telephones, Key card machine, photocopier with scanners, files and folders, stationary items, electronic safe etc. Without them you would surely face difficulties in your operations.

Let's start with EDC machine. You must be wondering, which machine is this. A true hospitality professional and hospitality graduate will understand, but if any other individual is reading this book, may not be able to understand.

Wait, I shall help you in explaining this. All those who use plastic money or so called Credit Card or Debit Card must have seen this machine. This machine helps in making payments or transactions when you don't carry or prefer to carry currency notes.

You need to procure this from any reputed bank such as Axis Bank, ICICI Bank, IDBI Bank etc., through your Finance department. Your Finance department has to fill and submit certain forms along with legal documents of the company.

Upon using this service, bank charges certain commission on the services rendered by the bank. The forms and documents have all details mentioned on them.

Earlier in our times, the bank used to charge 2% to 4% commission per transaction on VISA, MasterCard. The commission percentage on American Express (also known as Amex) machine was the highest and their EDC machine need to be procured separately, from American Express bank only. They used to charge 3.5% to 4.5% per transaction.

These banks take at least two weeks to install the machine at the site (at the hotel). These banks provide free paper rolls with the machine on monthly basis to the hotel without any charges or fees.

Once the machine is installed then you need to check that you get all major features with the machine such as Offline Sale, Online Sale, Reports, Pre-Auth, Batch close etc.

Next equipment is telephone. The telephones are nerves of the hotel. The mode of communication is telephone among the staff, with the guest, with the managers or any outsider. There is a separate room or area from where all telephone lines originate and from where all telephones are connected. This room has server which helps in tracking all the calls, whether the calls are incoming or outgoing, outside the hotel or within the hotel.

The technician who fixes the telephone set up in the hotel has to accompany the Information Technology personnel while installation and configuration. This would help in resolving any problem or issues later on.

Being a Front Office Manager you may decide on the extension numbers as well as guest room calling numbers or room extension numbers. You may decide on call holding music, call forwarding process, Wake call process, message, automatic answering process, call waiting process, outgoing call number or digit, operator extension, emergency number etc.

As a manager you need to check all the functions of telephone after set up, especially the guest room telephones.

Third equipment which comes in this chapter is, Key card machine which needs to be configured with your PMS. Please ensure while installation, that the machine is enabled with below listed features

a. Making new key
b. Making duplicate key

c. Deactivating the key or key check out
d. Reports
e. Login id should be as per shift of the person handling the machine
f. Calendar for counting the days and dates (helpful during activation of the key)
g. Configuration with the new lock on the door

Fourth equipment which is required for the operation is Luggage trolley. The trolley helps in carrying the luggage carefully and professionally .There are two types of trolleys available and procured by the hotels. One is Bird cage trolley and another one is Hand trolley.

Fifth equipment which sometimes Front Office has to operate, and that is Music System. Yes, this instrument or machine helps in maintaining a musical and relaxing environment in the lobby. Being a manager of the department, you may choose the music as per hotel location, hotel theme, size and décor of the lobby. Actually the music is played in the lobby to relax the environment and avoid certain unwanted noises of machines, telephones, people conversation etc.

Sometimes small things are also important for running the operations which should not be ignored such as stapler and pins, paper punching machine, thumb pins, pens, pencils, eraser, rulers etc. You need to keep such basic stationary items as well to show your professionalism.

Last equipment from this topic, which I would suggest, is Drop box, which can be made by the carpenter or you may also keep an electronic safe but it should have space on one of the sides to drop cashier envelope.

If you are getting it from the carpenter then it should have very strong lock and one set of three keys. Out of three keys, one should be with Accounts, second with Security and third with you.

****

CHAPTER NINE

C-Form Registration

Don't forget to get the hotel registered in local FRRO (Foreign Registration Regional Office), else you may fall in *deep shit*.

For the registration you need to register the hotel on Indian FRRO portal. It is mandatory for you to register on this before starting the operations. It is not at all complicated process. You just have to fill the hotel and company details, and submit the print out of the form at FRRO. Within one week or so, the hotel would be listed on Indian FRRO portal and staff can access the same through login id and password.

"I think I have touched and tried to cover the main areas and points for setting the department in the new hotel under opening phase.

****

I hope that this book would be helpful
to any new Front Office Manager in the future."
"ALL THE BEST IN PRE-OPENING AND OPENING"